THE CARING CANCER

Text by Therrie Rosenvald

Illustrations and Design by Marco Schmidt

3rd Edition 2009
2nd Edition 2004
1st Edition 2001

ISBN 10 Digit: 1-877063-03-7

ISBN 13 Digit: 978-1-877063-03-9

Published by
Astrology Art
24 Wallace Road
Beachmere 4510
Queensland, Australia

www.astrologyartpublishing.com

CONTENTS

PERSONALITY

HARD SHELL, BUT KIND HEART

Cancer, the fourth sign of the Zodiac, rules the House of Home and the heart of every Cancerian centers around the home and family life. The Cancerian planet is the Moon and in ancient time the Moon was considered the Mother of the Heavens. Cancerians represent the maternal characteristics, which makes them the most caring sign of the Zodiac. Cancerians have a natural ability to nurture others and a deep desire to protect the weak and helpless.

The Moon is also associated with fertility and indeed many Cancerians marry at an early age and take great delight in procreating. Soon Cancerians are proud parents of an impressive number of offspring. They take their parental duties very seriously and will do anything to protect their young ones. They must be careful not to appear too protective and smother their children.

The Cancerian is a traditionalist and with great zest and vigor they will make sure that long established family traditions are kept alive and the family history, sometimes dating back centuries, is handed down from one generation to the next. They can also be staunch patriots and will wave the national flag whenever an opportunity arises. The astrological symbol of the Cancerian is the crab and like the crab Cancerians may have a hard shell, but their interior is extremely soft. If their home life is harmonious the crab is a merry fellow and fun to be around. However, if things aren't going too well and someone has hurt their feelings Crabs may hide in their shells for days, even weeks.

Describing Cancerians as a bit sensitive is the understatement of the year. The scale of these people's sensitivity can reach into the stratosphere. One day they're kind, helpful and will listen to all their friend's troubles with great understanding. The next day they're bad-tempered, moody, and snappy and refuse to speak to anyone. What happened? Who knows... maybe someone made an unkind remark or didn't give the crab enough attention. Or maybe the moon has been reduced to a sliver in the night sky and Cancerians just feel very vulnerable at the moment.

The darker side of Cancer is that these people have a tendency to brood and will forever harp on about a tiny injustice done to them eons ago. No one can nurse a grudge as effectively and as long as Cancerians. It may take decades for them to forgive the most insignificant wrongdoing.

But sometimes Cancerians will stubbornly display their hard shell to the world precisely because they are so sensitive and their emotions often run away with them. To protect themselves they'll act tough and pretend to be hard as nails. They'll proclaim to everybody that they couldn't care less about anything. Don't believe it. It's all an act.

The Cancerian element is water and like all water signs Cancerians can't help feeling so deeply. They constantly swing back and forth on this emotional pendulum, from one extreme to the other. The plus side of this super sensitivity is that they can tune into their loved one's feelings without any difficulty. Because of their caring nature Cancerians are highly appreciated as partners and friends. Their intuition guides them through difficult times and is a key factor in reaching decisions.

In general Cancerians are good with handling money, but they like to be surrounded by beautiful things and won't hesitate to spend money for people close to them. However, they are very security conscious and saving for a rainy day makes perfect sense to them. Their yearning for security means that the Cancerian pantry is always well stocked. The Crab likes to be prepared for all occasions and enough food in the house will ensure the family's survival should any disaster strike at a moments notice.

The crab is a creature that moves between the land and the deep ocean. This also applies to people born under this sign. They take their earthly responsibilities, which represent their need for security, very seriously. But Cancerians also need time to nurture the depths of their imagination and secret dreams. Sometimes their longing to escape to the deepest waters of the oceans can no longer be ignored.

FEMALE

FROM LAUGHTER TO TEARS

You'll have trouble deciding if your Cancer girl is a gentle dream come true or a lunatic let loose on the unsuspecting male population. When it rains, she will drown you in her sorrows, when the sun is out, she will have you in fits of laughter. One minute she's gay, flirtatious and tender, the next she snaps at you with her crab-claws and then seems to sink in a bottomless pit of apparent misery. It doesn't take long to discover that the Crabette's moods are in sync with the changing face of the moon. A midnight stroll on the beach with the silvery moon shinning brightly will bring out her secret passions and dreams. In a matter of seconds she will transform into a mystical creature from another world.

The sign of Cancer represents everything maternal and the Cancer girl is synonymous with warmth, softness and femininity. She gently consoles, understands and nurtures whoever needs some tenderness, including the family dog. Whatever lies within her domain is kindly and generously protected with a fierce tenacity such as children, home, friends, allies and possessions. Anyone who disturbs the close circle of Cancerian girl's home will quickly feel just how hard those claws can pinch.

Her soft voice, the dreamy look and the gentle nature will quickly engulf both lovers and friends. However, it is not recommended to trifle with the Cancerian girl's emotions. She may never forgive you. The Cancerian woman carefully guards her own feelings. She needs to be strong because so much and so many depend on her. If her strength and integrity are threatened she may fight with bitter words.

Cancerians are passionate, but also possessive. Once the crab claws get a hold of something or someone they will not let go, sometimes to their own detriment. Thankfully crabs are gentle and easygoing creatures most of the time. Mothering is the Cancerian woman's great skill and she has the ability to soothe away all the ills of the world and create an atmosphere of serenity and security. The Cancerian woman will love, honor, protect and occasionally nag if things aren't shaping up to her expectations. This girl's emotions have incredible depth.

AN UNCOMPLICATED MAN...???

Spotting a Cancerian man isn't hard. It's usually that cuddly, well-nourished guy, grinning from ear to ear, with a cheeky twinkle in his eye. Somehow Cancerians even take on the physical attributes of the crab - a round torso and skinny legs sticking out. But don't forget there are also long and slim crustaceans in the ocean. That tall, skinny guy with the dreamy look observing everything from the corner may also be a Cancerian. The male Cancerian is a deeply romantic soul and will make a real effort to impress the female of his choice. This is definitely a one-woman man who will never have any trouble staying faithful.

In general Cancerians are a jolly bunch. They love to laugh and in the upturn of the lunar cycle they'll be in on any practical joke. However, if the moon is in decline the gentle smile of the Cancer man can be replaced with a wrinkled frown and his outlook becomes more sorrowful. At times he may become dominant, fussy and finds faults everywhere. During this phase little seems to satisfy this man and he may complain about everything and everybody. As the lunar cycle moves through different phases so does the Cancer man. By the time the new moon appears on the night's sky the Cancerian man may be brooding over the purpose of his life and why he should endure it. But as soon as the round ball shines down on him again the bounce returns to his step, he'll sweep up his beloved and head for the bright lights of the city ready for some fun and excitement.

The Cancerian man does not leap into life without looking where he's going to land. Actually, he doesn't leap at all. His is a slow and pragmatic pace, he likes to assess the situation before giving the slightest hint that he might be interested. This does not mean he's not a risk taker. Crabs never let on what their intentions are. The Crab purposely moves slowly and never in a straight line so that his goals and ambitions are not easily detectable. Cancerian men are family men at heart. They often marry young and become proud fathers of a whole horde of offspring. Their most endearing quality is their gentleness and tenderness, which makes them the most caring men of the Zodiac. This man truly blossoms in marital bliss.

AMBITIONS

TO GIVE TO FAMILY AND COUNTRY

At a first glance one would not think these people have any ambitions at all. Nothing could be further from the truth. Believe it or not but Cancerians are extremely ambitious. But they don't shout their wants and goals from the rooftops like some fire signs. Cancerians are very good at hiding their secret thoughts underneath that thick shell they carry around on their backs. Crabs are intensely private and they jealously guard their goals.

What would happen, God forbid, if someone were to discover what the Crab really wants? Cancerians go to great lengths to keep their intentions secret. They don't go blabbing what they want to do and which goals they want to achieve. Cancerians are fragile creatures and don't have much emotional strength to shrug off criticism, be it constructive or not. So as not to give the game away, Crabs seldom steer towards their goals in a direct line. They will circumvent the object of their desire many times before making a quick grab for it.

Cancerians are traditionalists and they hanker after the good old days. Often their ambitions centre on recreating the ambience and harmony of their childhood days. They'll yearn for that wonderful carrot cake their mother used to make. Cancerians want their children to be able to climb the branches of the big old Oak tree and run through meadows filled with wild flowers. They would do nearly anything to turn the clock back, at least emotionally. But their most treasured ambition is finding the right person with whom they can share togetherness and undying devotion to one another.

Creating such a happy world for their families doesn't come cheap and Cancerians will have to become quite worldly to make their wishes come true. They will fantasize about climbing to the top in the business world, becoming a leader of commerce. Some Cancerians also harbor some dark ambitions. They frequently fantasise about taking revenge for a wrongdoing. Of course, they never act on it, as Cancerians couldn't hurt a fly. They just keep on imagining it.

LOVE MATCH CANCER AND CANCER

Being caring, attentive and able to tune into their partner's needs will form the basis of this relationship. The gentleness and ability to give is the perfect recipe for a happy family life and a loving environment to rear children. Two crabs together feel secure in their love and enjoy each other's company immensely. They will happily potter around in the garden, share the housework and cook some fabulous meals for family and friends. But there is also a danger that they are too alike and start to mirror each other's weaknesses. A wrong word, a critical remark or thoughtless gesture may be misconstrued and suddenly some cracks begin to show in their happy world. Neither wants to take the first step towards reconciliation and a minor spat can become a major issue.

The Cancerian's primary ambition is to have a family and be an upstanding member of society. They are also highly patriotic and will salute the flag at every opportunity.

A Reflection of Their Mood

If they put their mind to it, Cancerians can be very smart dressers. Their outward appearance is often an accurate reflection of the state of their inner emotions. If the mood is good, they'll be walking tall and their evening dress will be shimmering in the bright light of the full moon. However, when the lunar cycle has changed and the chips are down, they'll slouch around the house in an old dressing gown with egg stains down the front, baggy pajama pants and Granddad's worn-out slippers with a hole in the toe.

The Cancerian style is traditional and soft. The female Crab looks best in feminine, soft lines that accentuate her voluptuous curves. Romantic styles with long, floating skirts that highlight the slim waists, are also very flattering. Male Crabs, with their strong upper torsos, make dashing figures in traditional blazers and flannels. In the classic dark suit, with jackets dropping easily over generous hips, they look a million dollars.

Cancerians like natural fibers and will stick to tried and tested styles. Although they may sometimes succumb to buying a gimmicky item, they prefer quality that lasts. Their color scheme is on the conservative side. By keeping the background neutral, they enjoy accessorizing their outfits with unusual pieces of jewelry. Many Cancerians are very good with their hands and are often accomplished dressmakers. Although Cancerians like to look good, fashion isn't all that important to them. If money is tight, it will be spent on more important things. The Cancerian mother won't buy a new dress for years because her children always need something that is more urgent.

Cancerians take great pride in their homes. Their furniture might have seen better days, but each piece will be polished like a mirror and a prized family heirloom. On the dining table meadow flowers, in a slightly chipped antique vase, will spread their scent throughout the house and in the kitchen, the delicious aromas from a roast in the oven brings back long forgotten memories of another era.

APPEARANCE

LOVE MATCH CANCER AND LEO

The masculine sun rules Leo and the feminine moon rules Cancer. They are the yin and yang of the Zodiac and this relationship has strong karmic connotations. Blending these opposed forces will lead to highly creative ventures. Leo is enthusiastic, confident and ready to tackle any problem. Cancer has to get used to Leo's exuberance. Otherwise, generous and strong Leo is just what insecure Cancer needs. Cancer is sensitive and will give Leo plenty of admiration and flattery. Leo's positive outlook will do wonders when Cancer's black moods strike. Cancer finds Leo's need for challenges and excitement a bit daunting. Leo seeks the bright lights and people while Cancer keeps the home fires burning for when Leo needs to retreat to lick his or her wounds.

Cancerians get emotionally attached to all sorts of things and often have trouble parting with a treasured possession even if it's outmoded.

CANCER LOVES TREASURE HUNTS

The Cancerians' career choice is often associated with their strong links to the past. They will spend many nights thumbing through old records and dusty books in search of information about a rusty war medal. On weekends they often travel through the countryside visiting flea markets or little old ladies to see if they can pick up an heirloom or little treasure for a song. Sometimes they're lucky and stumble across a particular valuable piece at garage sale or auction of a deceased estate.

Cancerians also make excellent teachers. They feel privileged to contribute to the development of young minds and take this responsibility very seriously. It will be the Cancerian teacher that many students remember fondly after decades. Another area in which Cancerians reap great rewards is in the hospitality industry. The barman, who listens to his patrons' many problems and has a kind word for every one of them, is most likely a Cancerian too. The army chef, who delights in offering the soldiers some good home cooking so that they don't feel homesick, may also be a Cancerian. After all, what is more nurturing than feeding the troops?

The health service is another area where Cancerians can make full use of their special ability to show empathy to suffering people or creatures. They thrive on caring for others and make excellent nurses, doctors, therapists or veterinarians. With their sensitivity and strong family values, Cancerians particularly excel as social workers and marriage counsellors. Careers that require a deep concern give Cancerians a feeling of accomplishment and job satisfaction.

Cancerian employers treat their staff like members of an extended family. They will nurture the talents and abilities and establish a close working relationship with each member. Be warned though, Cancerians are not pushovers. They will make the tough decisions if it is required. Someone continually ignoring the Cancerians instructions will soon be given the marching orders. The downside of Cancerian employers is that they can be moody. If an employee disappoints them they will not be able to forget easily.

LOVE MATCH CANCER AND VIRGO

Despite Cancer being emotional and Virgo analytical these two get on well together if they make an effort. It may take some time for Virgo to show emotions, but Cancer senses the passion beneath the reserved exterior. Stability is important for both of them and they will build a secure future. Virgo's biting critisim may cause some friction, but it doesn't stem from a mean spirit or attempt to be hurtful. Their partner's wellbeing is at the heart of the matter and if Virgo can make them aware of shortcomings they will do that, though their sensitivity is often more than a trifle lacking. This couple is comfortable and affectionate with each other. Cancer accepts and respects Virgo and Virgo's steadiness soothes Cancer's fluctuating up and down moods.

Cancerians like nothing better than to delve into long gone eras. They become ardent collectors of all sorts of memorabilia. Some even make it their career and become highly successful antique dealers.

THE MORE THE MERRIER

As the mother of the Zodiac, parenting comes naturally to Cancerians. Going forth and multiplying is burned into their brains. Having a family, with hopefully a whole horde of youngsters, is the highlight of their life. Cancerians know instinctively how to sooth the most unwilling infants. Nothing is more important to Cancerians than being good parents. Their children will never go to bed without supper, no matter how naughty they were. They will also never leave the house without a kiss and a cuddle, with the usual caution to be careful, and to call if they're late, even if that child has long celebrated his or her 30th birthday.

As this is a sign that holds on to traditional values, the Cancerian mother will most likely prefer to stay at home, at least while the children are still young and they can remotely afford it. The Cancerian father is as adapt at changing diapers as any woman and doesn't mind getting up in the middle of night. There is no other male as willing to participate so actively in raising a child as the Cancerian father. Cancerians are very lenient with discipline. They prefer to ask their children nicely to do something, and if they don't comply, the Cancerian parent will put on that sorrowful 'you've disappointed me' expression. It's amazing how fast the little ones learn to obey.

Cancerian parents can be highly ambitious for their children and may unconsciously steer them into a professional direction that is not of the child's choice. They often confuse what the child wants with what they want. Cancerians have a tendency to let the need to nurture get out of hand and they are sometimes accused of smothering their offspring. An extroverted, curious child, who wants to get out there and see what the world is all about, will give the Cancerian parents many sleepless nights and stress.

If Cancerians haven't got a family of their own, they will adopt one. They will pick up homeless kids from the street, feed them, and give them clean clothes and a warm bed to sleep in. All kinds of Charity organizations rely heavily on Cancerians putting their mothering instincts to good use.

LOVE MATCH CANCER AND LIBRA

Both Cancer and Libra are highly emotional, Cancer is deep and Libra is sentimental and happy-go-lucky. They both need lots of affection and will harmonise well in this respect. Libra is in love with romance and Cancer won't tire of showing it either. Cancer isn't as outgoing as Libra and an evening of togetherness means staying at home for Cancerians. But Libra needs people, excitement and lots of socialising. Also Libra is an incurable flirt and this will cause some major friction. Cancerians want to be the one and only for their partners and they will brood if the attention is turned elsewhere, even if it's harmless. They both adore a beautiful home and share many other interests. Libra will ignore Cancer's black moods and is a master at charming the gloomy Crab.

A happy home and family is the Cancerian's first priority. This is reflected in their eagerness to procreate the family line.

FRIENDSHIP

CRABS HAVE A JOLLY NATURE

Crabs don't make new friends easily. Firstly, because they're so involved in their close knit circle that they don't have time for other people and secondly, it takes a long time for them to trust someone outside the immediate family. They are shy and their pathological fear of rejection prevents them from making the first move. However, once they get over their reservations and forge a friendship, it will be long lasting and deep.

Cancerians make true and valuable friends. If a friend is coming down with a cold, Cancerians will get cough syrup, lemon tea and herbs from the health food shop, prepare lots of pots of tea and sit by their friend's bedside while they recover. If the friend's heart is broken, Cancerians will come rushing to dry their tears and tell them that nobody is worth this much pain. If a friend has just received a promotion or won lotto Cancerians will celebrate with them and make sure they get home safely after all those glasses of French champagne.

Cancerians invest a lot of time, effort and emotions into their friendships and they expect the same caring attitude to be reciprocated. A friend, who forgets the Cancerian's birthday or fails to send them a get-well card or bring flowers when they are ill, will deeply hurt the Cancer's feelings. Little things really count in a friendship with Cancerians. Anyone who ignores these little things is ignoring the Crab. Cancerians may never forgive or forget such crucial oversights. It is doubtful that they will ever resume a friendship with such thoughtless people. A hurt Crab can become quite snappy and may even retaliate with poignant, hurtful remarks.

As a water sign, Cancerians are very emotional people and emotions play a big part in any friendship. Once they've accepted someone into their inner circle they can be surprisingly candid about their feelings. There is also a jovial side to Cancerians. In the company of trusted friends, with a glass of good wine and tasty food, they come out of their shells and quickly become the life of the party. Cancerians need companionship, however, they would rather be alone than with someone who is not caring and considerate.

FRIENDSHIP

LOVE MATCH CANCER AND SCORPIO

When two water signs get together the many facets of emotions will play a huge role. Cancer's loyalty and devotion is just what Scorpio needs. Both can be possessive, though Scorpio's tactics are more ruthless. This pair is very protective of one another. Cancer admires Scorpio's strength, while Scorpio cherishes Cancer's commitment. Both are extremely intuitive and sense what will please the other. Cancer can handle Scorpio's demands better than any other sign. Scorpio can at times be just as moody as Cancer. Scorpio must take care not to be too pushy and make unrealistic demands. Cancer expresses love through gentleness, Scorpio through raw physical passion. This partnership has real intimacy, intensity, and depth. This is mostly a happy and loving union.

When the moon is full Cancerians become very sociable and seek out the company of friends. In general Crabs are happy go lucky people who enjoy a few laughs and interesting conversation.

HYPERSENSITIVITY IS A PROBLEM

Tensions, problems, strains or any other distress go straight to the Cancer's stomach. Beneath the hard Cancerian shell is a soft underbelly, literally. Ulcers appear and their sensitive digestive system is soon totally out of whack. On top of everything else during the lunar cycle their emotional well-being gets churned around and around like in a washing machine on the spin cycle. Life is not always easy for Cancerians.

No matter how calm and cool they appear, underneath the surface the Cancer's emotions are bubbling. They are highly susceptible to emotional upsets. A rebuff by someone close, or not so close, which would hardly cause other signs to lift an eyebrow, has long-lasting and devastating consequences for the Crab. They have a tendency to bottle things up and it doesn't take long for pessimism and stress to surface.

People born under this sign do not always communicate easily, which makes it difficult for others to offer support. This in turn gives Cancerians the impression that their friends and loved ones are uncaring and they suffer in deafening silence. It takes the patience of an elephant and a truckload of love to entice Cancerians out of their shells and by the slightest provocation they will quickly pull their heads back in again.

The other great vice in the Cancerian's health is food, lots of it and very rich. They not only cherish mama's home cooking, they also like the size of the helpings. Cancer rules the digestive system and too much of the good life will come back to haunt them in the early hours of the morning. Cancerians like to worry and food is also a great comforter.

Cancerians are one of the more 'rounded' signs of the Zodiac and sticking to a regular exercise program is quite a challenge for them. If they're not careful the waistline will disappear and the tummy will balloon out. Water retention is another Cancerian ailment and their drinking habits should be watched. A couple of days on a low-fat diet, a few laps in the pool, and a concerted effort to let go of grudges, will do wonders for Cancerian's physical and mental health.

HEALTH

LOVE MATCH CANCER AND SAGITTARIUS

At first glance Sagittarius may seem like a dream come true. They will sweep Cancer up in their exuberance and carry the crab along on a cloud of wishes and dreams and crazy schemes. Nothing is impossible for Sagittarius. A notion Cancer may take on for a while, but soon Cancer starts seeing the cracks and will have to douse the Sagittarian fires with buckets of the icy waters of reality. Sagittarius doesn't have a problem with Cancer's critical views, what Sagittarius can't handle is defeatism. The horse can and will change direction in an instant. Cancer takes life very seriously and yearns for steadiness and security. These are the very attributes that Sagittarius hates. The Sagittarian bluntness may also wound the crab. The horse needs freedom and the crab needs a home.

Like the tides of the ocean Cancerians are ruled by the moon and their emotions and moods mirror the lunar cycle.

WATER REPLENISHES THE SOUL

Crab people yearn for tranquility and inner peace. It is important for them to be able to escape the daily demands and where better to do this than on the shores of rivers, seas or oceans. Water is the Cancerian's element and they flock to it like seagulls. Riding the waves of the ocean, even if it's only in a swim ring or boogie board or just sticking one's big toe into the cooling waters, restores the mind and heart.

Secretly Cancerians dream of sailing the high seas and following the routes of the great captains in history, like James Cook or Marco Polo. Maybe they'll even discover an island that everyone has overlooked somewhere in the middle of the vast oceans and where no man has sailed before. Having their own boat or yacht would be the pinnacle of Cancerians' achievements and they would even move on to it permanently when they retire. But some dreams are not to be.

For Cancerians a holiday is very much a family affair. They will have planned it many months in advance and made sure there is a cot for the inevitable baby and Grandma's low-salt diet has been organized. It will offer each of the family members something special. Cancerians are attracted to holiday spots that give them a feeling of home. They'd much rather book into a family run Bed and Breakfast than into a large impersonal hotel close to all amenities.

Because of their strong need to be loved, Cancerians often agree to a destination for another's sake. This self-sacrifice doesn't usually pay off, as Cancerians won't be enjoying themselves. If things aren't what they had anticipated, crabs can get really into a foul mood. Cancerians aren't very good at hiding their annoyance and must take care not to spoil the fun for the others as well. But holidays also offer a chance to catch up with family and friends, to strengthen bonds of love and friendship and re-establish some lost connections. It is a perfect opportunity to repair frayed relationships. For Cancerians a holiday is not just to recuperate physically, but also emotionally. If their heart is healed, their body will repair itself.

HOLIDAYS

LOVE MATCH CANCER AND CAPRICORN

The attraction of opposites is strong and with each giving what the other needs nothing will be impossible for this couple. There may be some minor strife over the amount of time Capricorn spends at work. In the Cancer's view there is so much more to life than work and money. Needless to say that material things aren't very high on the Cancerian's priority list. But Cancer will soon learn that Capricorn's ambitions and hard work provide the very things that are so important to Cancer, namely a home and safety. Capricorn's brusque behavior is not always to Cancer's liking and Cancer's habit of retreating into their shell at the slightest criticism will annoy Capricorn. Capricorn gives Cancer security and Cancer softens the sharp edges of the goat.

Water is Cancerian's element and they like to spend as much time in it as they can. That dangers could be lurking beneath the surface doesn't worry them at all.

COME ON, LET'S PARTY 'TIL DAWN

The Cancerian's sense of humor is a matter of timing. If the moon is a big, beautiful round ball in the sky, Cancerians are ready to paint the town pink and blue and get bellyaches from laughing when told the most boring joke. Sometimes they can laugh themselves silly about things or situations others don't find amusing at all. If this happens, one only needs to look at the night sky for an explanation. However, if there is only a fine sliver of Moon left, no joke, no anecdote, absolutely nothing will be able to put even the faintest smile on the Crab's face. Not even the most brilliant comedian with an act worthy of a Grammy can entice the Cancer to an audible chuckle.

Cancerians can be wonderfully humorous. When they are in a good mood they can deliver jokes like no other and their funny stories will long be remembered. With their powers of observation and strong intuition Cancerians will pick up on the most camouflaged idiosyncrasies of their fellow man and poke some fun at it. But they are very sensitive people and will rarely laugh about other people's misfortune. They prefer to pick themselves as the subject of their jokes about shortcomings. This does not mean that other people are allowed to make fun of Cancer.

Crude and sexually explicit jokes are not the Cancerian's style. If their humor does include gender relationships and interaction, it will be very subtle and mostly in good taste. Jokes about family life or family members don't go down very well with the Crabs. It is best to stay clear of mother or mother-in-law jokes if one wants to remain on friendly terms with Cancerians.

When Cancerians make an effort to be funny, they are hilarious. Slapstick comedy doesn't appeal to them. They enjoy a quick wit and humor that isn't immediately obvious. With their loved ones gathered around them, Cancerians can entertain everyone with an endless stream of jokes and a zany sense of fun. That crazy lunar laugh starts in the belly, rolls up through the chest, gushes out of the mouth like a torrent and thunders through the stillness of the night.

HUMOR

LOVE MATCH CANCER AND AQUARIUS

This match is made everywhere else but in heaven. The Aquarian's detached, intellectual nature will make emotional Cancer insecure. In turn Cancer's clinginess restricts Aquarius' freedom. Aquarius is fiercely independent and while roaming the world, or at least the city, obligations are easily forgotten. Cancer will construe this as being uncaring. Aquarius has a nimble mind and has countless different interests. Cancer is mainly interested in creating a happy home life with lots of little ones running around. But for Aquarius, who wants to save the world, domesticity can be a hindrance. Cancer is easily hurt by the Aquarian criticism. All is not lost as sensitive Cancer shares many of Aquarius's idealistic views and will freely engage in humanitarian causes.

When the moon is a perfect round ball the quiet Crabs switch to party mood and their crazy 'lunar laugh' echoes through the night.

HAVE A POSSESSIVE STREAK

For Cancerians love is very serious stuff. It is the culmination of an unusually long courtship and hours and hours of mutual exchange of thoughts. It is the celebration of a commitment and the means of procreating, thus ensuring the continuance of the family line. For Cancerians, the unification of the body is also the unification of the spirit. Love is the ultimate prize, and not to be taken lightly.

Considering this, one would think that all Cancerians enter the state of matrimony as virgins. Not so, however, they don't hop from one relationship to the next. Occasionally, they do like to break out of their own restrictive environment and start partying, usually around the time when there is a full moon. When they are in a good mood and have had a glass or two, they can be immensely charming and witty. The flattery starts rolling off their tongues with ease. That mischievous twinkle in their eyes, the sensual soft touch and the lusty body language are enormously seductive. However, they do put an end to frivolous behavior when they are looking for Mr or Ms Right.

When Cancerians want to get serious, there is nothing straightforward about their love tactics. They'll take a step forward, turn, take three steps to the left, then two backwards, turn again and one right, and another forward. This will go on for quite a while. In many instances, prospective lovers get so annoyed that they simply walk off and look for a less complicated companion. Cancerian's greatest fear is opening up emotionally and sexually to someone else. Their feelings are so fragile, that even a simple remark can make them retreat into their shells for another long sulk.

For Cancerians, making love is about feeling safe. It is about letting someone else see what is hidden under their thick shell and not being judged. Sex and love cannot be separated in the Cancerian's mind. However, they are considerate, gentle and giving lovers. They sense their partner's sexual needs and with their acute sensitivity, will try to give complete satisfaction.

LOVE MATCH CANCER AND PISCES

These two will think that all their Sundays have come at once. Like two peas in a pod, soulmates and the perfect match would aptly describe the relationship between Cancer and Pisces. When the sun shines they'll be skipping through paradise, when the clouds appear they'll be drowning each other in rivers of tears. Cancer and Pisces are all about emotions, some would say that the emotional bond between these two is a touch overbearing. Both are caring and supportive and instinctively meet each other's needs. Actually they try so hard to please one another that they tend to ignore their own wishes. Too much unselfishness can be tiresome. Some "Me" time never hurts. Cancer is more materially minded and yearns for a secure home to which Pisces adds the spiritual atmosphere.

Once Cancerians have a hold on something or someone they won't let go even if they risk losing a claw.

MARRIAGE

GOOD AT THE SILENT TREATMENT

The very best foundation for a family is of course marriage. Therefore, Cancerians are quite agreeable to tying the knot as it gives them a sense of completeness. People born under this sign are often eager to marry and many enter the state of matrimony at a young age. Cancerians yearn for deep love and once they've found it, they're not going to let it go easily. Many Cancerians marry their childhood sweethearts. They often make a commitment without ever having experienced any other relationship.

The caring nature of a Cancerian comes to the forefront in marriage. They are highly protective of their spouses, sometimes to the point of smothering them. They'll do everything to keep their beloved safe both emotionally and physically. They usually have the latest security device installed on all the doors and windows.

Cancerians are deeply devoted to their partners and will lavish all their attention on them. The Cancerian husband will bring his wife a cup of tea to bed every morning even after many years of marriage and willingly shares household chores. The Cancerian wife will warm the bath towels and have a separate cookbook with all his favorite meals and create a warm and loving home. However, all this love and attention and "where are you going, dear?' isn't always appreciated by more extroverted signs. Sometimes Cancerians overdo their caring and nurturing. A Sagittarius or Gemini spouse may soon feel like they can't breath anymore. If they try to shake free of the crab claw, which has his pinchers firmly clutched around their arm, Cancerians immediately feel rejected.

A hurt Crab is very bad company. They'll sulk, refuse to communicate and retreat into their shell for weeks. Trying to make up with Cancerians is not an easy task. They never, ever forget. At the smallest sign that their spouse is again yearning for some freedom, they will immediately bring up the past transgression and go into their sulk routine for another month. But it's not all bad news being married to a Cancer. The positive side is that they are highly sensitive and can easily tune into their partner's emotions. If their loved one is hurting Cancerians will be there for them.

MARRIAGE

LOVE MATCH CANCER AND ARIES

When the fires get out of hand one usually douses it with water. This can also happen in a relationship between Cancer and Aries. Cancer sometimes needs to douse the fires of Aries' exuberance. This is not always a bad thing because Arians tend to leap into life without looking where they're going to land. Cancer's caution will ensure that the landing spot is, if not pleasing and profitable, at least not detrimental. Arians are full of ideas and plans and they can't wait to start new projects. But Rams are sprinters and not endurance runners, so the exuberance may soon puff itself out and then Cancerians have to finish the task. In love Aries is aggressive and loves to flirt. This will get up Cancer's nose and they get defensive, moody and cranky. Tolerance is the key.

Wounded crabs will retreat to their hiding place for days. They'll refuse to talk to anyone and won't come out until they're ready.

A HOME FOR ANYTHING LOST

Stray dogs, cats and birds instinctively find their way to the Cancerian's doorstep. Any creature that is sick, injured, and too old or has a family too big to take care of by itself will tread a well-worn path to the Cancerian's house. Even the odd goat will seek refuge.

Cancer is the mother of the Zodiac and all species sense that Cancerians are only too willing to mother them in their hour of need. Cancerians will readily put down a bowl of milk and hand out bones and doggy biscuits to the starving and forsaken, treat the injured and make room for another arthritic old cat. Animal welfare centers are filled with Cancerian volunteers and these organizations probably couldn't exist if it weren't for the tireless efforts of people born under this sign. Cancerians have a strong need to nurture the vulnerable and protect the weak. To save a fellow creature or at least alleviate its suffering comes naturally to the Cancerian character. Crab people may be moody at times, but they won't mind getting up every two hours to bottle-feed an orphaned baby animal.

The Cancerian's animal family easily outnumbers their human family. The unconditional love animals give soothes Cancerian souls. They also believe that caring for an animal is educationally valuable as it teaches their own children commitment and responsibility. They particularly favor raising children and young animals together.

Cancerians don't usually have exotic pets as they don't see animals as status symbols and being able to earn some extra income from breeding is not paramount in their minds. Actually, Cancerians take more of a shine to the moggies and mongrels of this world. Cancerians like cats, but if they had a choice they would probably prefer a dog. Dogs are more emotionally responsive than cats and Cancerians love the constant canine companionship. In the Cancerian household one finds a colorful array of pets. Rabbits will be housed on the back veranda. The hamster occupies the laundry and the tortoise and tree frog have settled in nicely in the bathtub.

PETS

LOVE MATCH CANCER AND TAURUS

Earth and water always go well together. Taurus and Cancer are both sentimental and homebodies. Taurus' down to earth nature is a good balm for Cancer's fluctuating moods. Though Taurus is not always the most diplomatic person in the world and has a habit of speaking his or her mind. Cancer being hypersensitive will get hurt when faced with the Taurean's no-nonsense approach. Taurus gives Cancer's emotional life some steadiness and Cancer will gently entice Taurus to occasionally make some changes in life. As both are giving souls their love life will be more than satisfactory. Cancer appreciates the Taurean dependability and will respond with loyalty. Both signs value emotional and financial security and their interests and goals are complementary.

With lost and abandoned animals Cancer's strong need to nurture definitely comes to the forefront. They willingly go without so that they can feed all the hungry animals arriving at their door.

SAVE FOR A RAINY DAY EARLY ON

Intangible wealth is far more important to Cancerians than just bricks and mortar. They are more interested in creating a happy family life than fattening the bank account. But they learn early that money does provide security and Cancerians are very security conscious. They like to know that in the future when they may have a spouse and six kids that they can get by. So Cancerians start to accumulate wealth early in life.

By the time Cancers marry and start having kids a sizeable nestegg will already be in the bank and before the kids hit their early teens there will be a generous college fund waiting for them. Cancerians have a good head for business and will turn nearly anything into a successful venture. Their interest in human nature serves them well. They have a great understanding of people's needs and an ability to meet them. With their sixth sense Cancerians detect popular crazes or fads long before anyone else. This great sense of timing allows them to buy in early, make a killing and get out of it again before the bottom drops out of the barrel.

They also use their legendary intuition well in commercial deals and know exactly when to buy and when to sell and when to walk out. There won't be many scoundrels, who can pull the wool over the Cancerian's eyes. They'll sniff out a dubious deal a mile away and know exactly when their opponent is bluffing. Although Cancerians will strenuously deny that they are lucky Lady Luck does have a habit of smiling on them in very odd ways.

Cancerians sometimes come across their fortune by mere chance. They may inherit Great-Uncle Joe's house and find a long forgotten original painting of one of the great masters in the attic. Or they discover a valuable piece of furniture or jewelry in a junk shop or at a garage sale. Cancerians have a knack of spotting a bargain among other people's junk. Their strong connections to the past come in handy when visiting antique auctions. They can easily differentiate between a reproduction and an original. Their only problem is that they tend to hoard and have trouble letting go of an exquisite piece when it's time to resell it.

WEALTH

LOVE MATCH CANCER AND GEMINI

Air tends to evaporate water and if they're not careful the love between these unlikely characters may too evaporate quickly. Cancer is all about feelings, family and security. They want to know where they will live next year and preferably the years after that too. In other words Cancerians have a close attachment to their homes, just look at all the crabs that carry it on their back. Geminis find emotions totally confusing and they'll ignore them as best as they can. The world is Gemini's playground and they can't wait to get out and explore every corner of it. Gemini's independence, restlessness and flippant approach to love will unsettle Cancer. Gemini needs to treat Cancer with more sensitivity and Cancer should enjoy the fun Gemini's lively mind creates.

Cancerians learn the value of a dollar saved early in life and they quietly fill one piggy bank after another. By the time they reach adulthood they've squirrled away a sizable fortune.

FOURTH HOUSE

HOUSE OF FAMILY AND HOME

The Fourth House is dedicated to the family and the home. This, figuratively speaking, is where life begins. Within the family home the foundation of the person we will one day become is established. It creates the building blocks with which the future is shaped. If the atmosphere in the family and home is positive and loving each member of the family unit will be endowed with a phenomenal strength and resilience, which will carry them through all ups and downs of life.

If, however, there is strife and conflict instead of love and understanding then the members of the family have to overcome great hurdles on their journey through life before they can grow positively. This highlights the enormous responsibility new parents must accept. They not only have to cater for the physical wellbeing and growth of the child, but they are also responsible for its emotional and mental development. Therefore the Fourth House is often also known as the House of the Mother, the Parent or Nurturer.

That this important house has been entrusted to Cancerians will surprise no one who is related or befriended with a crab. Cancerians embody the very essence of family life. It is sacred to them. They live and breathe it, which is clearly visible by the quantity of their offspring. No sacrifice is too large for the sake of their children. They won't mind running around in the same old clothes year in and year out so they can educate each child properly. Cancerians often dedicate their entire lives to the nurturing of their families. If they don't have a biological family of their own, or their spouse has firmly declared that two children are enough in this day and age, Cancerians will adopt or create an emotional family by taking in every stranger or lonely person and stray animal that crosses their path.

People born under this sign, or have a strong Cancerian influence in their astrological chart, are the guardians of many family units. They keep track of all the different branches of a family clan, remember the names of every great aunt and uncle, five degrees removed, whom they married and how many kids they had. Cancerians are the ones who visit the seniors of the family in the nursing homes and always have something good to say about a person at their funeral.

Many Cancerians take up the hobby of establishing the family tree. They painstakingly research over many years the family background of every person with the same surname in the telephone book. They make late night calls to total strangers in foreign lands and ask them about their grandmothers, who they married or if they had any illegitimate children. They probe into who begat whom on both sides of the family until they have established a reasonably chronological family history.

By this time Cancerians are not only familiar with where each brother or sister of their great-great-great grandfather eventually ended up, but also how that branch of the family prospered or declined over the centuries. Needless to say that establishing a fairly accurate family tree isn't a cheap hobby. It is time consuming and the expenses over the years can run into the thousands. If these family snoops really get into things they'll self-publish a book with the history of the clan and try to flog it to all the relatives at weddings, funerals and baptisms.

Tangibly speaking the Fourth House also refers to the actual structure of our home, namely the buildings and it has been noticed that some Cancerians are quite capable of accumulating many "homes". In other words they build up an impressive portfolio of real estate. No doubt, lots of relatives will be attending this crab's funeral.

Another aspect of this house is the spiritual and emotional home we carry within us, our self. A home, be it physical or spiritual, should become our sanctuary, the place we go to lick our wounds when things go wrong, where we feel safe and accepted. This is the place where all pretenses can be peeled back. It is where the real person with all the positives and the negatives is exposed and still accepted without prejudice. If this inner home is in sync with our environment and our emotions then we feel grounded and at peace within ourselves.

MOON: PLANET OF EMOTIONS

Despite the fact that our closest planet is only a rocket flight away the moon continues to intrigue us. The moon orbits the earth every 27.3 days; hence we speak of a lunar cycle. It is the lunar cycle that has such a dramatic impact on Mother Nature, beasts and humans. It haunts our fairytales and the ghosts of dark secrets seem to hide behind its shadows. The echo of lonely wolves howling at the full moon in dark forests sends chills up anyone's spine. The tides of the oceans as well as the emotional wellbeing of the inhabitants of the earth are all under the moon's spell.

This is the planet that rules our emotions and it also rules the sign of Cancer. Cancerians are all about emotions. They wear their hearts on their sleeves. When the moon is a big round ball in the sky nothing is impossible for Cancerians. Their happiness is infectious and they'll be bringing home small gifts for their partners and children. This is not the time to waste with problems, they boast, this is the time to celebrate being alive and content. The champagne flows freely and as the promises roll easily off the tongue the laughter and jolliness sweep through the house.

But the moon stays in any phase only for a couple of days, so the time of fullness and plenty, of laughter and frivolous antics is limited. With the changing face of the moon the Cancerian mood too starts to dip. They slowly slip down the emotional slope with limited chance of halting or slowing their descent. Before long Cancerians drop emotionally from euphoric highs to the cold depths of the ocean floor.

Their sadness is heart wrenching and they drown you in a river of tears. A careless word, a critical look or an innocent oversight becomes the crux of utter misery. They pull their shell over their ears and refuse to listen to any explanations or reason. Somehow the crab's feelings have been mortally wounded. Thankfully this phase too is passed quickly and in between these two extremes most Cancerians are more or less emotionally balanced, kind and easy to please, until the next lunar cycle sweeps over them.

CANCER BIRTHDAYS

22.06.1949	Meryl Streep, Actress
23.06.1400	Johannes Gutenberg, Inventor of Printing Press
24.06.1942	Mick Fleetwood, Fleetwood Mac
25.06.1903	George Orwell, Novelist
26.06.1892	Pearl S. Buck, Author & Humanitarian
27.06.1880	Helen Keller, Deaf & Blind Academic & Author
28.06.1491	Henry VIII, King of England
29.06.1963	Anne-Sophie Mutter,violinist, Berlin Philharmonica
30.06.1975	Ralf Schumacher, Formula 1 Racing Car champion
01.07.1961	Princess Diana, Princess of Wales
02.07.1877	Hermann Hesse, German Writer
03.07.1962	Tom Cruise, Actor
04.07.1927	Gina Lollobrigida, Actress
05.07.1911	Georges Pompidou, French President
06.07.1946	George W. Bush, US President
07.06.1922	Pierre Cardin, Fashion Designer
08.07.1839	John D. Rockefeller, Oil Magnate & Philanthropist
09.07.1956	Tom Hanks, Actor
10.07.1926	Fred Gwynne, Actor 'Herman Munster'
11.07.1934	Georgio Armani, Fashion Designer
12.07.1937	Bill Cosby, Comedian
13.07.1942	Harrison Ford, Actor
14.07.1918	Ingmar Bergman, Swedish Filmmaker
15.07.1606	Rembrandt, Dutch Painter
16.07.1872	Roald Amundsen, Norwegian Explorer
17.07.1934	Donald Sutherland, Actor
18.07.1918	Nelson Mandela, Civil Rights Leader & first black South African President
19.07.1834	Edgar Degas, French Impressionist Painter
20.07.1919	Sir Edmund Hillary, Mountain Climber
21.07.1952	Robin Williams, Actor & Comedian
22.07.1890	Rose Kennedy, Matriarch
23.07.1892	Haile Selassie, Emperor of Ethiopia

LaVergne, TN USA
18 January 2010
1676LVUK00001B

* 9 7 8 1 8 7 7 0 6 3 0 3 9 *